Marketing Untangled Series

Competition Untangled

The Small Business & Entrepreneur's Guide to Knowing Your Competition

By
Thoranna Jonsdottir

ISBN: 978993592346
ISBN-13: 978-9935-9234-6-2

Already available in the series:

Marketing Untangled: *The Small Business & Entrepreneur's Map Through the Marketing Jungle*

Target Groups Untangled: *The Small Business & Entrepreneur's Guide to Finding and Knowing Your Ideal Target Groups*

Available in print and on Kindle: amazon.com/author/thoranna

Don't miss out on the meaty info you'll find in the next books in this series! Simply sign up at Marketing-Untangled.com for updates on these next books:

Branding Untangled: *The Small Business & Entrepreneur's Guide to Building Your Brand*

Marketing Communications Untangled: *The Small Business & Entrepreneur's Guide to Choosing the Right Marketing Communications*

Marketing Systems Untangled: *The Small Business & Entrepreneur's Guide to Setting Up an Effective Marketing System*

Dedication

For Kalli, Ísold Saga, and Ísak Máni,
without whom all of this would be pointless.

Contents

Acknowledgements

There are a few people who I would like to thank.

My husband and children are always going to be at the top of my list, and then my parents and little brother. Their unwavering support for everything I do, and their patience when I get yet another idea and always strive for more. As we say in my house, "When Mom is happy, everyone is happy." That's just how it is. :) My family's never-failing belief in me, even as I lose faith in myself, is an endless source of strength; as is their support as I continue to seek the best way to be the best I can be.

My clients throughout the years deserve a big thank you for appreciating what I know and do, and for acting on it. Seeing you use what I have taught you and getting results with it is the reason I do this. It's the reason I am getting these books out, even though life has gotten in the way, and my journey has developed and changed since I first began working on the training program – which is the basis of these books.

Endless thanks to my Runa who always reminds be to be just who I am and that I am enough. When many others want me to be more sterile and boring to be "professional," she reminds me that there is only one me and that is a gift. Being professional is not the same as being boring. You can be professional and competent and still have fun and enjoy life! And boy do we enjoy it when we're together.

Thanks to my editor, Livingstone, for his patience during the oh-so-very-long break from starting the work on these books, until I finally got up off my ass to finish them. They have really been ready for a long time, but hey, life's what happens while you are making other plans, so there we are.

Thank you, Mummi, for helping make this vibrant pink marketing nerd look good.

I have been blessed with a lot of good people in my life who have inspired and supported me. The list would be too long to present here...you know who you are, and you know I love you. However, I do want to mention a few key clients throughout the years that have meant the world to me and who have become dear friends; people such as Davíð, Dóri, Martha, Herdís, Heiðrún, Katrín, Rut, and Ingvar and many more that prove to me how awesome it can be to work with great people!

Xo
Thoranna

The Marketing Untangled Series - Why I Wrote It and How It Works!

Through all my years of working in marketing – whether at agencies, within businesses, or as a consultant, teacher, or mentor – things always come back to the same basic foundational things again and again. People are anxious to see results, and therefore tend to want to dive into tactics. What advertising to do, which social media to be on, what to say, and so on.

Well, here's the truth of the matter: tactical decisions in marketing cannot be made without a solid strategy. A rock-solid foundation. This is why, without exception, I have always had to bring my clients and students back to the foundation. The marketing strategy. Because these foundations will then tell you what marketing tactics to use and what you should say in your marketing messages.

I have also found that marketing is as much about organisation, research, and project management as it is about strategy and tactics. Because without this underlying backbone of organisation and planning, your efforts will be unfocused, inconsistent and sporadic, which is not conducive to good results.

This is why I started to develop materials and processes to lead my clients and students through, allowing them to build a solid marketing strategy and program that works. To build a system for your marketing, a marketing machine, that you can then run to get the customers and business that you want. I call it my map through the marketing jungle – my step-by-step process for untangling the marketing mess (hence *Marketing Untangled*). It consists of five steps, and each of these steps is the subject of a separate book in the *Marketing Untangled* series, as well as the topics covered in the modules of my online training program – *The Marketing Untangled Training*.

I'm not going to pretend that I came up with all this myself. I didn't. These things have been researched, studied, tried, and tested in business and academia around the world. The strategies are the same ones underlying the success of businesses we see all around us: Apple, Coca-Cola, Nike – but also thousands of small- and medium-sized businesses who have grown to where they want to be, and perhaps did not want to become the next global corporation. What I have done is to distil all this knowledge and experience into a practical, jargon-free, step-by-step process suitable to the needs of entrepreneurs and small and medium businesses. What you need to know; nothing more – and nothing less – in an easy to digest and easy to use manner. No fluff, no academic mumbo jumbo.

The purpose of these books is not to make you a marketing expert. Nor should you necessarily want to be one. However, if you own or run a business, marketing is something you must have a good understanding of.

Why? Because marketing is at the heart of business. Marketing is your business. It is the lifeblood of your business. Marketing is what gets customers and without customers you don't have a business. It is all about understanding the needs of the customers and fulfilling those in a profitable way – that is the definition of marketing. As Al Ries said: *"Marketing is what a company is in business to do. Marketing is a company's ultimate objective."*

Peter Drucker had it spot on: *"Marketing is the distinguishing, the unique function of the business...Marketing is not only much broader than selling, it is not a specialized activity at all. It is the whole business seen from the point of view of the final result, that is from the customer's point of view. Concern and responsibility for marketing must therefore permeate all areas of the enterprise."*

I'd ask whether you still think marketing has nothing to do with you – but then, you'd probably not be reading this book. ;)

The other reason for having a good understanding of marketing strategy and the various tactical options out there is because when you do buy marketing services or hire marketing staff, you need to be an informed buyer. You may not want to become an expert in social media or search engine optimisation or any of the other tools and tactics available to you, but you should have a basic understanding of what they are and what they are supposed to do – so that you know what services you are buying, what skills you are hiring, and whether they are working for you.

Since my life as a marketing expert started at the dawn of this new century, I have seen way too many great businesses fail to reach their potential and many fail completely. I have seen entrepreneurs with an incredible amount of passion for what they do get absolutely nowhere. I have seen fantastic products and services fall by the wayside. In the majority of those cases, it is because the team lacked understanding of and skills in marketing. A 2012 literary review at the University of Iceland[1] showed without a shadow of a doubt that marketing orientation (looking at business from the point of view of the customer *à la* Drucker) and marketing skills are the single biggest business success factors, irrespective of business size. This is simply something people cannot ignore and if left unattended, your business will curl up and die.

However, we can't all become marketing experts and we can't all spend years getting marketing degrees (and many would argue their limited usability in the marketing trenches anyway). We need the most effective injection of marketing knowledge and understanding possible, and that is exactly what

---

[1] Eysteinsson, Friðrik, and Guðlaugsson, Þórhallur Örn, 2012. Literature review at University of Iceland. Presentation by Friðrik for Dokkan in February 2012, *Hvers vegna ná sum fyrirtæki viðvarandi betri árangri en önnur?* Or: *Why do some companies consistently perform better than others?* http://www.slideshare.net/Dokkan/fridrik-eisteins-feb2012.

Marketing Untangled is all about, and that is exactly what I want to give you. Nothing more. Nothing less.

This book is about the second of the five elements involved in building a solid marketing strategy and program: knowing your competition. In my previous book, *Target Groups Untangled*, I discussed the importance of knowing your audience (also called your target groups). In that book, I showed how to determine who your target groups are and what you need to know and understand about them to effectively reach them. This is the first element in building a powerful marketing strategy.

Your marketing strategy is really, really important and worth doing well, because it lays a solid foundation for all your marketing efforts and makes all your marketing activities much more focused and efficient. One could say that your strategy work is about 80% of your marketing, so if you do your job well with this stuff, the other 20% will be so much more effective.

A solid marketing strategy also makes all your marketing decisions so much easier. It works a bit like a compass. When you are not sure what to do, you can go back to your strategy and it will help you make a decision. If things fit within the strategy, you are off to the races; if not, then you will have a clear reason why and be able to let that idea go without having to worry if it was the right thing to do.

But knowing your target groups and competition does not a marketing strategy make. There are three pillars to your marketing strategy, and then – and only then – will you have a powerful launchpad for your marketing communications. These pillars are: knowing your target groups, knowing your competitors – and based on these two – creating a strategy for the brand you want to build.

The second marketing strategy pillar, and the subject of this book, is knowing and analysing the competition. Your business does not work in isolation, and to get results, you need to take the environment in which it operates into account. That environment is influenced in large part by your competition – and therefore knowing your competition is crucial. It is not so much that the knowledge is part of your strategy, but that it *informs* your strategy.

A side note: Your competition is not the only thing in your business environment that needs to be taken into account when formulating your strategy, but it is definitely one of the biggest factors. In the reader resources at thoranna.is/competition-untangled-reader you will find a bonus report on general market analysis that should give you an idea of what else you should analyse.

One of the most important things knowledge of the competition gives you is that it allows you to differentiate yourself – to be able to give a confident answer when someone asks, "Why should I buy from you rather than them?" That differentiation then becomes a core element in your brand, the third pillar of your marketing strategy, and the subject of *Branding Untangled*.

Your brand is the mental and emotional associations people have with you, your business, product, or service. In other words, your brand represents what they think and feel about you – and make no mistake, this is arguably the single most important thing in marketing. Why? Because people buy based on thoughts and feelings – and your brand is what determines what they think of you and how they feel about you (and hence whether they buy from you). Also, having a strong and interesting brand – being different and distinctive from the competition – is an absolute necessity to cut through the noise of a crowded marketplace and get noticed. In *Branding Untangled,* I lead you through the strategy for successfully building a brand, deciding what you want people to think and feel about you – and how you can then build that brand in the hearts and minds of people out there.

Once you have those solid foundations for your marketing strategy, then, and only then, can you start thinking about what marketing communications channels, tools, and tactics to use and what to say to your market. Your target groups will tell you where you can reach them and what marketing messages will be most effective, and your brand (which needs to be different and distinctive from the competition) will help you get noticed and get people's attention.

In part four of the process, and the subject of *Marketing Communications Untangled,* we look at how your marketing communication activities need to support each other and create a holistic program to get people to buy from you.

People don't just see your ad once and jump straight into buying. You need to make sure that you have the right tools to attract them and get them to buy, so selection of marketing communications tools and making everything work together in a systematic fashion is vitally important. In the book mentioned above, I also introduce a multitude of marketing communications tools and tactics at your disposal, thereby helping you choose the ones that are right for your business.

The final part of an effective marketing program is setting up a system. Knowing all about your target groups and competition, having a kick-ass brand strategy, and knowing exactly what you want to say in your marketing messages – and what channels and tools you are going to use to get your message out there – is useless if it doesn't actually get done.

When you are running a startup or small- or medium-sized business, it is easy to get distracted and not get your marketing done. This is deadly. The only way to get things done is by getting organised. This is covered in *Marketing Systems Untangled*. It's all about getting your marketing organised, taking all the work you did on strategy and marketing communications and using that as a "springboard" to set up a plan – finalising that map through the marketing jungle so that you can then start to follow it step-by-step to your money tree.

If the target groups, competition and brand are the pillars of the launchpad for your marketing communications rocket, then the marketing system is the fuel that makes sure it actually gets off the platform and keeps soaring!

As you can see, although I've broken the process into five steps and five separate books, these elements do not work in isolation. They all need to come together to form a marketing strategy and program that works and gets you customers. I therefore encourage you to read the other books in the series as they come out and to use them to put your marketing machine together.

To further help you gain an overview of the five parts of the *Marketing Untangled* Series, I would like to give you a free copy of the first and original book, *Marketing Untangled: The Small Business & Entrepreneur's Map Through the Marketing Jungle*. This book acts as an introduction to the series and gives you a more detailed overview of the five elements of the process and how they fit together. You will find your copy in the reader resources for this book at thoranna.is/competition-untangled-reader. Get in there now to create your account and get your free access!

One final thing. Things do not happen by themselves. In order for the materials in this book to actually be helpful, they must be put to use. It is not enough to just read it. I suggest you open your calendar or diary and set aside time regularly to work on your marketing, whether it is working through this book or any other marketing activities that need doing. More often than not it is not the most clever individuals in the world who achieve success, but rather the ones who take action. Knowledge is not power unless it informs action. And the fact is most people simply don't act, they simply don't do. Don't be one of them. Take action!

Ready to take your marketing to the next level? So how about we start by getting to the bottom of what those pesky little competitors are all about, so you can kick them to the curb and rock your market!

1. Read This First – About Your Competition

"Competition is always a fantastic thing, and the computer industry is intensely competitive. Whether it's Google or Apple or free software, we've got some fantastic competitors and it keeps us on our toes." - Bill Gates

I agree with Bill Gates. Competition is a good thing. It keeps us on our toes – keeps us alert, awake, and always pushing our boundaries. It is also an indicator that the market you are in is actually worth being in. If there is no one out there doing anything similar to what you are doing, it is more likely than not that the reason is simply that people aren't interested in what you're offering (this isn't always the case, of course, but it is certainly very frequently the way things are).

Why do we need to analyse the competition? Can't we just do our thing, do it well, and not think about what others are doing?

The basic reason for analysing your competition is very, very simple. You have to be able to answer this question: "Why should I choose to do business with you rather than anyone else?" If you don't know your competition and what they are up to, you won't be able to answer that question. And if you can't answer this rather straightforward question, then why on earth should anyone do business with you?

You need to stand out in the marketplace, be distinctive, and cut through the noise. If you don't know what the competition is like - how are you going to distinguish yourself from them?

You will also find that you can learn a lot by analysing your competition. You can learn from the things that they do well and borrow good ideas from them. You can also learn from their mistakes. What, for example, are they doing wrong or simply not well enough? What makes you think, "I can do better than that!" And in that observation lie valuable opportunities. If you don't know what your competitors are up to, you are going to miss out on those opportunities.

There's something else worth mentioning here, too: you don't want the competition to one day sneak up on you, overtake you, and as a result your business falters and ultimately closes. We all know those kinds of examples, and in hindsight we shake our heads and think, "They should have known better." But don't be too sure you know better - unless you have explored and analysed your competitors in an objective fashion and are systematically and regularly monitoring them.

There are a number of other reasons for analysing and monitoring the competition. It helps you keep abreast of what is happening in the marketplace, and helps you stay one step ahead. As Philip Kotler, the godfather of modern marketing, said: *"Poor firms ignore their competitors; average firms copy their competitors; winning firms lead their competitors."*

These are only a few reasons, but hopefully they are big enough to make you realise that competitor analysis is necessary for your marketing. Mind you, you probably wouldn't have picked up this book if you didn't think there was something to it. Am I right? ;)

So what are we going to cover in this book? Here you go:

We will establish who your competitors are, which ones you need to watch closely, and which ones you only need to keep an eye out for.

We will discuss the need to know your competitors and what it is exactly that you need to know about them.

We will explore where you can get information about the competition.

We will get a clear overview of the competitive landscape, enabling you to spot opportunities in the marketplace.

I will give you ways in which you can continue monitoring your competition.

Finally, we will discuss how and when to review and go over your competitor analysis.

Make notes regarding the information you uncover in your analysis. I suggest making them in electronic format and keeping them in a safe place where they can be easily found and updated (Google Docs and Sheets is a particular favourite of mine!).

Make a "date" with your competitor analysis and keep it. Don't let other urgent things get in the way of doing this – remember, don't underestimate the impact your competitors could be having on your bottom line!

Competitor analysis does not have to take ages. How long it does take depends on many factors, such as how many competitors you have, how well you know them already, and what your market is like. Access to information can also vary greatly between markets and industries and either make your job easier or harder. It's also good to remember that this is the only time you have to dive quite this deep. In the future, you just have to review and amend regularly, adding and updating things based on what you learn.

Through the years, a lot of my clients have said to me, "Thoranna, I don't need to do this analysis of the competition, because I know all about them." Hey, I'm working with grown ups. I can't force them to do competitor analysis. But then they come to a point where either they start thinking it might be wise to listen to me, or they get to a point in their work where they realise they need to know their competition better to make decisions on things like branding. So they finally do the analysis, and without exception they come to me raving about what an eye-opener it was, how much they learned from it, how much it helped them, the opportunities they uncovered, and on and on. So don't do what they did and waste time thinking you know all about your competitors – go do the research. ;)

This book is short, but deceptively so. It is packed with useful stuff, and there is some valuable additional information in the reader resources at thoranna.is/competition-untangled-reader. The reasons I have put these resources there, rather than in the book, are twofold: firstly, it means I can easily add to them as more things come to light, are pointed out to me, and so on. Secondly, because it allows for hyperlinks to further resources.

Don't let the shortness of the book itself make you believe that this is not important stuff. It is very important. I promise you – it is very, very useful to analyse and monitor your competition! Now go forth and dissect those little buggers. ;)

2. Who Are Your Competitors?

There are always a deluded few out there claiming that their product or service is *so* unique that there is no competition. Bah – humbug! Trust me, there is **always** some competition. Before you and your product or service came into the marketplace, your potential customer found some way to meet their need or solve their problem – the same needs you claim to fulfil and the same problems you solve.

How did they do that? What options – other than what you are offering – can meet their needs and give them the same benefits? Think carefully about this, talk to people and ask them, and always remember to keep an open mind. When people are considering buying your products or services, what are their options? What else may they consider doing or buying? Keep in mind that convincing yourself you have no competitors is a delusion that will harm you in the long run. Be relentlessly objective about analysing your competition.

Start by looking at the competition in the widest sense of that word. Your competition is *anything that meets the same need or solves the same problem for your target group or groups as your product or service does.*

As I discuss in my book on target group analysis, *Target Groups Untangled*, people don't care at all about what you do or why you think you're special. They only care about themselves. I am not being mean – this is just human nature. People always need to know what your product or service does for *them* – what's in it for *them*.

The fact is that the customer always has choices. In fact, doing nothing is always an option for them, too – to not buy anything at all and just ignore their need or problem, or hope it goes away on its own. If you are clear about the needs your product or service meets, the problem(s) it solves, and the benefits of using your solution, you will be in an excellent position to determine how else that need can be met, and therefore who your competitors are.

As with everything in marketing, you need to think about this from the customer's viewpoint – not your own: "I am a potential customer; I need A, B, C; what are my options? I can buy from you; I can buy from someone else; I can do things myself; or I can just solve the problem in some other way. Oh – and I can choose to do nothing at all!"

EXAMPLES:

Websites

Say you create websites for businesses. The potential client can choose a multitude of CMS systems (content management systems), including open source like Wordpress, Joomla, and Drupal, or proprietary ones serviced by website providers. Then they have a wide array of choices as to who can set up their website, from solo website designers to big agencies and everything in between. They can also do it themselves with user-friendly options like like Wix, Weebly, or Squarespace. They can even decide not to have a website. A few years back, a lot of small business owners thought that having a Facebook page was probably enough, and that it could replace having a website (as we have seen how Facebook's organic visibility for pages has developed, that was not a good idea, apart from many other reasons to have an actual website).

Apps

If you have an app aimed at teenagers, the pool of competitors is very wide and very deep. You could say that anyone that tries to get teens to spend their disposable income with them is in competition with you. Not just other apps, but also movies, computer games, music, and a wealth of other things. When teens spend their pocket money, they consider an awful lot of things that money could be spent on – why should they choose your app (or any other product or service that targets teens)?

Let's do a little exercise to explore your competition in the widest sense. Grab a piece of paper and jot the following things down as they apply to your products or services:

Estimate the total number of competitors in the market. Just a ballpark figure. This can be tricky. For some this may be a huge number. For others, this may be a very clear-cut, small number. Are there just a handful, or are there tens, hundreds, or perhaps thousands of competitors? For artists and designers, for example, there may be hundreds if not thousands of competitors when looking at things this widely.

Do you know of any potential competitors that may be entering the market in the near or not-so-distant future? If so, note them down, because you will need to keep an eye out for them. Do you know of anyone that is getting ready to invade the market right away? Have you heard or seen anything? It is important to be wide awake and aware of what is going on in the marketplace.

Consider indirect competition. Are there possibly any indirect competitors that may make moves into your market? They may be making use of strengths in certain areas, such as distribution channels, a strong brand, or something else – and they may be using those strengths to move closer to your market and become more direct competitors. Keep your eyes open. I have a feeling that before 2007, Apple wasn't really the major focus of mobile phone manufacturers' competitor analysis. Nokia, Motorola, and others probably simply considered Apple to be a computer company and had no inkling that iPhones would become the must-have thing.

Do you have any way of knowing how the market is divided among the players in it? Who is the biggest, and who is the smallest? Or are they all similar in size? It can be useful to look at this, because this will affect the dynamics of the market. A few large players may not collude formally, but they will cause the market to move slowly for their fear of disrupting the balance. Meanwhile, a lot of small players or a mixed bag of players is more likely to make for a much more dynamic and exciting market, with competitors trying to outdo each other (to give a very general example).

List all the competitors you can possibly think of – and then even more. Really stretch your brain. If you are in a market where there are hundreds, if not thousands, of competitors (such as for designers and artists, coaches and speakers), you may be able to group them together in some way, or you can pick out those that you feel are most similar to you. Also, pick out those competitors you admire and aspire to be like – you can learn a lot from studying these competitors, after all.

List ready? Great...onwards, then.

Now you are going to narrow it down a bit. Identify the competitors that meet the following criteria:

Those that meet exactly the same *needs* as you do. Take out any indirect competitors, unless you think there is a great risk of them entering the market. Just focus on the ones that meet exactly the same needs or solve exactly the same problems. Be careful though: if you have a pizza place, your main competition is not just other pizza places, but also restaurants in your area within a similar price bracket. That luxury *à la carte* restaurant down the street, however, would not be classed as a main competitor, even though occasionally some of your regulars may decide to treat themselves there. ;)

The competitors that have the same *target groups* as you. If you have listed competitors with totally different target groups, take them out of your list – unless you have reason to believe they will make a move on your target groups. For example, a luxury hotel would not worry about the hostel down the block (but the hostel may want to monitor whether the hotel company wants to cover the market by using their knowledge and resources to open a competing hostel). If you are not sure who your target groups are, you need to determine this. You may find my book on target group analysis, *Target Groups Untangled*, useful for that. You can find information about it in the reader resources at thoranna.is/competition-untangled-reader.

The competitors operating in the same geographical market(s). A restaurant in New York doesn't really have to worry about a restaurant in London – unless the New York restaurateur has reason to believe the Londoners are building a worldwide chain, and the Big Apple is the next stop. A local florist in Reykjavik doesn't worry much about florists in Tokyo. Even if you have an identical business – with an identical target group – if you are in different geographical areas you needn't worry about competitors in non-overlapping geographical markets. (Internet-based businesses, of course are different – in which case you need to examine which geographical markets your competitors are targeting). However, if you know of someone in your business niche somewhere out there that is doing great things, I do recommend you analyse and follow them to learn from them and get ideas and inspiration for your business. ;)

The competitors that are comparable to you in price and quality. This is called *positioning* in the market, and those that have a similar positioning are often referred to as a *strategic group*. Skoda would not consider Ferrari a competitor – and you could actually debate, to an extent, whether they fulfil the same needs. Skoda is a much more practical choice that gets you from A to B, but Ferrari more likely than not fulfils needs related to status and self-expression. In the spirit of this example, those competitors on your list that are in a completely different price or quality category can be taken off the list, unless you have a specific reason for keeping them – such as a high likelihood of that business coming out with another product or service to cover your strategic part of the market. For more on positioning in the marketplace, you may want to check out my upcoming book *Branding Untangled*. You will find information about it in the reader resources at thoranna.is/competition-untangled-reader.

Great! Now, how many competitors do you have on your list?

If you have 10 or fewer – these you will examine more thoroughly and monitor as you move forward with your competitor analysis.

If you have more than 10, you may want to choose the most significant 5-10 competitors. Make sure you keep any that are important, but you also want to be realistic in how much analysis you can do. You need to use your judgment here. You should keep any competitors that:

Lead the market – those you can learn from and are likely to impact the market in a way you need to be aware of.

Are most like you, as they will be your closest competitors.

Are likely to be doing something of strategic significance in the near future, so you need to keep an eye on them.

This should leave you with a list of the competitors to examine in more detail, which you will do in the next chapter.

Action Points

- Estimate the total number of competitors in your market.

- List all of the competitors you can think of.

- Whittle them down to a maximum of about ten, which you will analyse further and monitor as you move forward

3. Know Your Competitors

"So it is said that if you know your enemies and know yourself, you can win a hundred battles without a single loss." - The Art of War by Sun Tzu

Now, I am not saying that the competition is necessarily your enemy. In fact, you'd be amazed at the opportunities that can arise in working with your competition in various ways. But the part about knowing your enemies and knowing yourself is crucial. (The whole thing about knowing yourself is something I cover in more detail in *Branding Untangled*, mentioned before.)

But what do you need to know about them?

Let's go through a number of things you may want to examine about your competition. Make a note of all this in a safe place which you can easily access, and in a format you can quickly amend, and add to it as you go along. You might feel that gathering all this information is a lot of work, and that we are delving quite deep (maybe too deeply!), but I promise you it is worth it and you will find this useful in so many ways.

One more thing: I suggest you revisit this and review and update your competitor analysis at least once a year; you may want to do this more frequently if you are in a dynamic and fast-moving market.

Here we go...

Products and/or Services

Make a list of all the products and services the competitor provides. If they are highly diversified into areas that are not in competition with you, just list the product or service groups in the categories that do compete with what you're doing. But within your common market, make sure you are aware of everything they offer.

Consider this example. Suppose you run a local restaurant and the local hotel also has a restaurant – as well as as spa and meeting services. Provided that the restaurant is not too different from you in terms of price, class, and quality, the hotel restaurant presents competition. However, you don't offer a bed to sleep in, meeting facilities or a spa, so you don't need to analyse those in any detail. However, be aware that they may be able to fulfil certain combined needs, and therefore might have an edge over you precisely because of their range of services. For example, someone who is staying at the hotel may find it convenient to just have dinner there too, thereby giving the hotel restaurant an advantage over you. You, after all, have to drag them out of the comfy hotel and into your place.

A highly diversified business with their fingers in many pies may have problems juggling all the different sides to the business. So they may not be as focused on the product or service that is in competition with you and this may provide some opportunities. However, they may also have more resources and therefore be a stronger competitor. Their risk is also distributed over various categories, whereas you may have all or most of your eggs in one basket. On the flip side, if you have your fingers in many pies, but the competition can focus their efforts on fewer products and services, they may have the upper hand.

Website

Note the URL for their website. If they offer an RSS subscription, put their website URL into an RSS reader such as Feedly (www.feedly.com) – and, subscribe to their newsletter so you get email updates straight from the competition (as I discuss below)! In this way, you are subscribed to any updates on their website so you will know when they change anything or add things. If they have a blog, make sure you get that emailed to you when they publish a new post, so you don't miss anything. The website also provides a wealth of valuable information about them, so study it carefully and check it regularly. How often depends on how dynamic your market is. (Don't rely completely on RSS or other methods to notify you of any changes, so make a note in your calendar to check their websites).

Social Media

Make a note of all of your competitor's social media profiles. Are they on Facebook, Twitter, LinkedIn, YouTube, Instagram, Flickr, Pinterest, Tumblr, Snapchat, or any others?

Like them. Follow them. This is one of the best ways to monitor your competition. Create a list on Twitter: put your competitors on a specific list and hide it, and so on. Make sure you make these kinds of lists private – you don't want others to know you are monitoring them and you don't want your lists to bring attention to your competition (that's up to them to do). ;)

On Facebook, you can use the "Pages to Watch" feature on your own Facebook Business Page to monitor their Facebook pages.

Other Listings

Are your competitors listed anywhere else? Booking sites? Directories? TripAdvisor? Google Business Listings? Are they on any map services? Make a note of all of this, and if there is a way to get notifications about them, make sure you sign up for those.

Email List

Do your competitors have an email list? Subscribe to it! Ideally, use an email address that doesn't have your business domain on it. You can always get a free Gmail account and then forward that to your main email account to disguise your identity. ;)

Competitor Size and Sales

Find a way to evaluate the size of your competitors' businesses, both individually and also relative to each other. Now, this can get tricky. Information is often not lying around just waiting for you. But the good news is that there are different methods out there that can help you with this. For example, you can certainly get a good idea of the size of the business from the number of employees they have. This information is often readily available on their website or LinkedIn Company Page.

Even more useful is information on their sales and turnover. If they have published annual reports, you can get this information. In some countries (my own Iceland, for example), you can get a copy of annual accounts for all registered companies by just paying a small fee. Research what this is like where you are, check with the Companies Registrar, tax authorities, or other official bodies that may have information about this. Annual accounts can provide a wealth of information about the competition. You may also be able to find clues in importation documents (customs documents, for example) or even in the media. You may also find research companies that will sell you this kind of information. This is often expensive, and you need to evaluate carefully whether the money is worth it.

Finally, if possible, it is useful to know their market share. Now this can get very, very tricky. Sometimes you can access this sort of information through research companies. Often this takes quite creative research on your part, and this research will vary greatly from country to country and industry to industry. A creative client of mine in the small Icelandic market managed to calculate the market share of the major players in the laptop market by studying customs reports and seeing how many laptops were imported. Combining this with other data he had internally, such as sales figures, he got quite a good idea of how the market was distributed. Can you find any inventive ways to figure this out for your own market?

Even if it is just information about the number of employees, this will still give you some idea of size and relative size in your market, which is useful for understanding market dynamics.

Position in the Market

It is important to get a feel for each competitor's position in the market relative to other competitors. This can be a big eye-opener and uncover many opportunities, as well as give great insights into market dynamics and behaviours. So think about it – which one of these definitions best applies to each of your competitors?

Leading: Are they a market leader? Do they have a lot of influence on other companies' success or actions? An example is Apple's positioning in computers and technology. The iPod, iPhone, and iPad are examples of innovations that have heavily influenced other competitors and greatly changed their respective markets.

Strong: Are they merely a strong competitor? Can they do their own thing, for a shorter or longer period, making important business decisions without having to seriously consider the competition? Or are they sensitive to their competitors' actions? Or perhaps they have been in the market for a long time and have gathered a lot of trust and goodwill.

Good position: Perhaps they are just doing well and making good money. Do they have anything special? Do they have a niche that allows them to fairly easily strengthen their position in the market?

Defendable position: Perhaps they can just defend their position. They may be doing well enough to keep going, doing okay, no major weaknesses – but also not doing anything special; in which case, this state of affairs can provide you with opportunities.

Weak: Are they simply weak? Will they either have to seriously start doing better or just leave the market? Could they perhaps be wiped off the market completely?

New entrant: Are they new in this particular market or new in general? Based on what you have seen so far, what do you expect them to do in the future? Do they look like they are going to be strong or weak?

Competitor Strategy

Where are they going? How do they want to position themselves in the marketplace? What are their future plans? Do they want to be the biggest and strongest market leaders? Does it look like they are focusing on a niche? Does it look like they will be expanding either to new products and services or new markets? Are they aiming to have the lowest prices and get a lot of business, or do they perhaps charge a lot and only need and want a small – but lucrative – part of the market?

Have a look at their annual reports, their website, etc., and see if you can find anything about them in the media (or anywhere else that you can think of) which can give you clues as to what their strategy is. Make a note of everything you find out.

Differentiation

How are your competitors planning to be different and distinctive in the market? You must have a good idea of who they want to be because you will want to be different from them. And you can't make decisions about how you are going to be different unless you know what they are like.

Consider the mobile phone market. Apple goes for the trendy, cool, design-conscious attitude. Samsung is a bit more techie. Then you have Blackberry (or should I say had? ;), which seems to focus very much on the business market. There are also phones like Huawei, which are cheap and cheerful. And even Caterpillar has a phone that can take all the hard knocks you expect from a Caterpillar product.

The point is that each of them has their own "thing." Rather than creating a me-too with those already in the marketplace, find your own "thing"; something that makes you different from your competitors such that you boldly and distinctively stand out. But you can't be different unless you first know what your competitors are like – so study them!

In another book in the Marketing Untangled series, Branding Untangled, I delve deeper into this whole idea of standing out in the marketplace. This will not only help you differentiate your business, product, or service, but also help you understand what your competitors are up to – so you can find your own place in the market.

Price and Quality

How does your competition position itself with regards to price and quality? Do they plan to be the cheapest – and are perhaps willing to sacrifice quality to ensure this? Are they expensive and top-quality? Is there a discord between price and quality? Perhaps they are charging too much for poor quality, which will most likely bite them in the behind eventually. Or do they seem really inexpensive compared to their quality? That can be a double-edged sword.

Yes, it delights the customers, but a low price can also signal that the quality is lower than it actually is and deter consumers from buying. The car market is a great illustration of the interplay between price and quality. Are your competitors a flashy, expensive Ferrari or perhaps more practical – but premium – like Volvo? Perhaps they want to be a reliable, no-nonsense kind of car that just works and you pay for what you get, like a Skoda. Perhaps they just want to be dirt cheap?

It is a very useful exercise to map your competition on two axes of price and quality - and see where you fit on this "map."

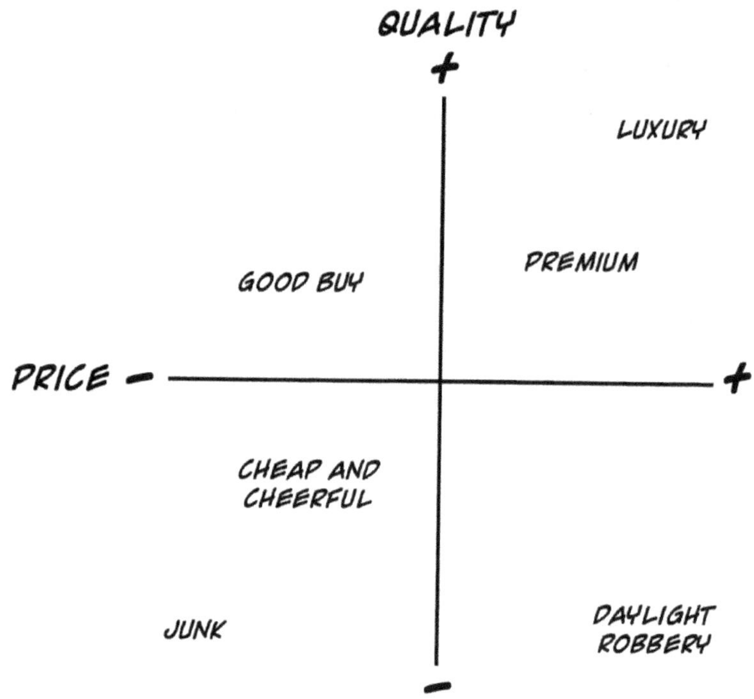

Discounts, Payments, etc.

How does the competition price their products and services? What are their discounts, terms of payments, financing, and so on?

It is very important to understand your competitors' pricing strategies and make a conscious decision about your own pricing strategy relative to theirs. Pricing is also a strong indicator of how you position yourself against competitors in the market. Do you plan to always be a bit more affordable, or do you want to indicate that you are of a better quality – by always being a little bit more expensive? The pricing structure of your competition is, as you see, very important.

How easy it is to get your hands on this information depends on your business and industry. Sometimes you can see the prices online or in a store; for others you may have to have someone "spy" for you by calling them up. This may be particularly tricky with professional services where the price can be a matter of agreement on a project-to-project basis, as well as in business-to-business (B2B) markets where there are tenders and things like that. You may need to think outside the box, do a bit of digging, and even enlist the help of others to do some spying for you by posing as a potential client to uncover this kind of information.

Target Groups

What are the competition's target groups? Are they all the same as yours? Are some of them the same and some not? Which ones are the same? Which ones are not the same? Understanding this is based on a clear understanding of who your target groups are. If you have not determined, defined, and analysed your target groups, you may want to check out another book in the *Marketing Untangled* series titled *Target Groups Untangled*. You'll find more information on that in the reader resources at thoranna.is/competition-untangled-reader.

Brand – Image and Reputation

What is the image and reputation of your competitors like? What is their brand? As discussed above, basically a brand is what people think and feel about an entity – in other words, what comes to mind when someone thinks of something, whether it is a company, product, service, or person.

A clear understanding of your competitors' brands uncovers opportunities for differentiating yourself from them and informs your own branding efforts.

What do people say about your competitors? Look them up on Google and see if people are talking about them online. Talk to people around you. What do they know about your competitors? What do they think about them? This will help you get a picture of how competitors are perceived.

If you want to gain a better understanding of branding, check out *Branding Untangled* when it comes out in the *Marketing Untangled* series.

Sales and Distribution

Where and how do your competitors sell their products and/or services? Are they online or brick and mortar stores? Do they have their own brick and mortar locations, or are there middlemen like retailers or affiliates? How is the product or service delivered? Online (digital products) or offline? Are goods delivered to the customers' door or do they have to go to a store to get them? Do your competitor's sales and distribution channels impact their business health? Do they have a prime location in town or are they way out in the country? How easy is it for customers to reach them? What are their facilities like? Are they just local? Are they in more locations across the country – or perhaps global? Do they have partnerships that give them greater access to customers?

Have a careful look at all this – and more – because you may have to get to their level. Or you may uncover an opportunity to serve your customers through other channels. A good example of discovering new opportunities is established companies – that have been around for a long time – ignoring the internet or failing to do well enough in this digital sphere, with new competitors coming into the market and mastering the internet. In this way, the younger, smaller businesses gain great competitive advantage (Amazon vs. Barnes and Noble, anyone? :))

Marketing Communications

What marketing communication channels do your competitors use? Do they use social media? What is their website like? Do they have a mailing list – or send direct mail? Do they use traditional advertising media? If so, what kinds – and where do they advertise? Ask questions like these to get a good sense of the marketing communications your competitors use.

Do you have any way of knowing what is working for them and what isn't? There could be great opportunities here to outdo the competition wherever they are underperforming.

Competitive Advantage

What do you do better than the competition? What do they do better? Could they copy what you do without much effort? What gives them their competitive advantage? Can you outperform them in their areas of competitive advantage – or can you find another way to outdo them? Something that sweeps them aside in your wake, something you can do better, something that may matter more to the customer?

Sometimes businesses that have been around for a long time can get a bit complacent – a little easygoing – and may not always meet the needs of their customers in the best possible way. This may yield opportunities for you.
Note that a true competitive advantage is something you do better than the competition and is *sustainable*. Good service, trust, quality, and speed of service are often unsustainable sources of competitive advantage. It is not impossible, but very, very hard to maintain them over long periods of time and they are generally not something you can truly own. Think about airlines, for instance. One of them offers something extra like more legroom and that works well for them. What do the others do? Increase their legroom. The initial innovator is back to square one. Then they go ahead and offer the ability to completely lie down during flight, so you can sleep. If that works well and draws in business you can bet that it won't be long

until the others do that, too. Things can often be easily copied and all you end up with is businesses leapfrogging each other.

Finding a meaningful competitive advantage is therefore a very tricky thing but can also be very valuable. There can be natural sources of competitive advantage, such as owning diamond mines (not many of us have those!) or oil wells. But you can also build a competitive advantage - for example, through the network effect of everybody using your product or service. As an example, Facebook has built a huge competitive advantage as a social medium because everybody and their brother is on there (and what good is a social medium unless the people you want to socialise with are there?). It will be very hard for another social medium to topple them, because they have a vast number of loyal users. Amazon is another example. It is now so entrenched in the marketplace, that it would take an extremely strong competitor to come into their space and make any kind of serious dent in the Amazon business. For some companies, a strong and distinctive brand may be their most valuable competitive advantage. This is the case for Apple.

Similarities

What are the similarities between you and your competitors? Do they matter? Should you be changing something that may be too similar? This could be something simple, like not using the same brand colors as your main competitors - or something more complex like not offering the same kind of payment plans. Can you outdo them on those points of similarity - and how? Go over anything that may matter to your customers and look at how competitors are doing it, and how you are doing it. Then see if you can do better on those points.

Learn

- What can you learn from the competition? What are they good at? Do they have a weakness that you can take advantage of? ;)

- Now then, with all of that out of the way, here are a few more things that may be relevant to your competitor analysis:

- What is the company structure like? Is it flat or does it have a large pyramid or hierarchy? Are they bureaucratic - with lots of red tape, or are they lean, mean, and dynamic? What does that mean for you? Are they leaner, meaner, and more dynamic than you are? If so, what can you do about it?

- What are their general production capacities and skills like?

- How much excess production capacity do they have, if any? What does that mean for competing with them? Are they likely to expand their business to use this production capacity or sell off some of their production resources? Are they struggling because of unused excess capacity?

- Do they have easy access to - and strong relationships with - retailers or wholesale companies?

- What do your competitors do about their competitors? How do they react? Are they perhaps watchful and proactive in dealing with their competitors - or lazy and unattentive? This will affect how they respond to your moves in the market.

- What is their range of product and services? Are they highly focused on a specific niche - or do they have a very diversified business? What does that mean for them, and what does that mean for you?

- Have they been through mergers and acquisitions? How has that affected their business? Or may mergers or acquisitions be looming?

- How are they doing financially? Are they strong? Or are they teetering on the brink of bankruptcy?

- Do they have international connections, and if so, are they strong? How do they, or could they, use them?

- How profitable are they?

- What is their cost structure? In other words, what are their main costs? Do they have a lot of burdening fixed costs, or do they have a lean operation where they can easily react to circumstances?

- Do they outsource and keep things flexible? What does this mean for their business?

- Do they have great in-house capabilities in areas that really matter?

- Do they invest heavily? Do they have strong investment capacity? What does that mean for you?

- How would changes in quantity or price of sales affect them? Can they meet increased demand?
- Can they bankroll a loss? How would price changes affect their profitability?

- Cost of finance: is it different for them than for you? What does that mean?

- Investment possibilities: could they invest in other companies? What could that do?
- Business connections: do they have them? Which ones? Do they use them? How? Are they better or worse connected than you are?

- How tech savvy are they? Are they still in the Dark Ages or do they use all the latest technologies for the betterment of their business?

- How innovative are they? Are they stuck in a rut, or constantly developing, getting new ideas, producing innovations, etc.?

- What is the main source of their profits?

- Do they have easy access to the media, in order to get media exposure?

- You will find this list, and more points, in the reader resources for this book at thoranna.is/competition-untangled-reader.

- Make a note of all your observations regarding the above points and consider what that means for you. What problems can you see? What opportunities have you uncovered?

- You will want to go over this regularly. How often depends on how dynamic the market is. In slow markets with few players, you may get away with reviewing this only once a quarter – but in fast markets, such as many retail markets, you may need to have your eye on the ball each and every day.

- Do you have something more that you think would be useful to think about with regards to the competition? Let me know and I'll add it to the list in the reader resources at thoranna.is/competition-untangled-reader!

Action Points

- Go through all the points above and make notes on anything relevant to your business.

- Check the list in the reader resources for more points (and let me know if you think of any that you feel should be added). ;)

- Make sure you keep this information in a secure yet easily accessible place, where the information can be easily updated (Google Docs is a personal favourite of mine).

4. Where Can You Get Information about the Competition?

There are lots of places where you can get information about your competition. Below you will find a few useful things to get you going and ideas of where you can get competitor information. In this list, for the sake of simplification, I have combined methods of gathering initial information with ways to monitor the competition on an ongoing basis. In a later chapter, we will discuss ongoing competitor monitoring and review.

To keep this list as up-to-date as possible, I have put the list in the reader resources for this book (where you will find the list below as well as a collection of more links to useful resources). Grab your free reader membership at thoranna.is/competition-untangled-reader!

- The competitor's website and blog – so often overlooked. Go through all of it – regularly!

- Check out all their social media profiles, such as Facebook, Twitter, LinkedIn, Instagram, YouTube, Pinterest, Snapchat etc.

- Follow them on social media wherever they are, such as Facebook, Twitter, LinkedIn, Instagram, YouTube, Pinterest, Snapchat etc.

- Put their Facebook pages in "Pages to Watch."

- Make a list on Twitter (private).

- Do a Google search for them – regularly! See what comes up (for example, have they been actively using Google pay per click ads?).

- Get a hold of their marketing materials and continue to collect them in an *organised* manner. You can collect screengrabs of their online activities, have a scrapbook for any print material, have a hidden playlist on YouTube and Vimeo if they put their videos on there, and so on.

- There are services out there that can monitor your competitors' advertising for you, but they can be expensive. Check them out for your market and see if they are worth using.

- In some countries, annual reports for certain forms of companies are a matter of public record and obtainable by paying a fee. See if this applies in your country. This can be very interesting to read and can give you great insight into your competitors' businesses.

- If applicable to your kind of business, visit the competitors' businesses regularly. I have a client who has a restaurant and has identified four main competitors. Each week she will go eat at one of her competitors' restaurant, so she experiences each competitor about once a month. If you can do anything like that, do it!

- If for some reason you can't do it yourself, get someone else to visit the competitors' businesses and report back to you. Suppose you sell wedding dresses – that's a fairly small market and it probably wouldn't go unnoticed if you turned up regularly at your competitors' locations to try them on. ;)

- Call the competitors' businesses to get information to see what their customer service is like – or get someone to do it for you, if you can't do it yourself for whatever reason.

- Do a bit of market research and ask people about your competition, particularly if they do business with them. Why do they do business with them? If they don't, why not?

- Not quite as formal or neutral, but still worth doing: ask your business partners, people in your network, and current or past customers of yours, about the competition – whether they have done business with them and what their experience was like.

- Be part of any kind of professional or trade associations or societies where you rub shoulders with others in "the biz." This will help keep your finger on the pulse of your competition.

- Set up a Google Alert to get current updates about your competitors.

- Read their articles, news about them, press releases, and anything else you can find on them.

- Be on their mailing list, get their newsletter, etc.

There is a wealth of information out there. Check out more ways to learn about the competition in the reader resources at thoranna.is/competition-untangled-reader, and if you know of more that you think should be there, drop me a line at competitionuntangled@thoranna.is and I will add them to the list!

5. The Competitive Landscape

Once you have gone through the competitor analysis, it can be useful to step back and take a helicopter view of it. You may find that competitors can be divided into groups. These could be referred to as strategic groups – just like we talked about previously with regards to price and quality. Often when you start analysing the competition, you will find that you can divide them into such groups. In other words, these are businesses that are alike in some way. It's useful to visually map these groups to get a better overview of the competitive landscape. This can help you understand your place in the market better and may uncover interesting opportunities. ;)

Let's use a couple of examples to explain. Please note: these examples are purely fictional and are merely put forward to demonstrate how one could possibly map the competitive landscape in the marketplace.

The competitive landscape of gyms and exercise facilities in your local town could look something like this:

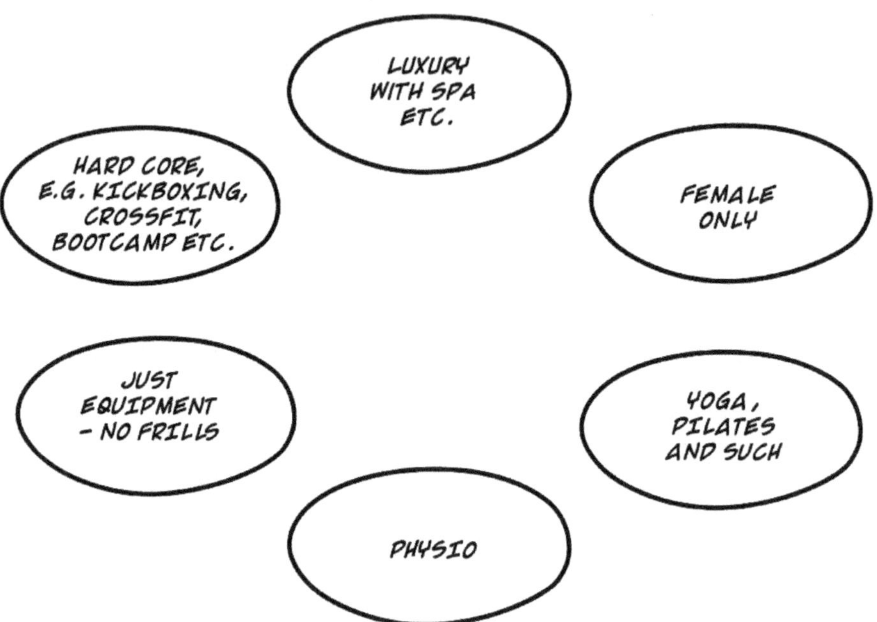

An agency selling website services may get a map for its market looking something like this:

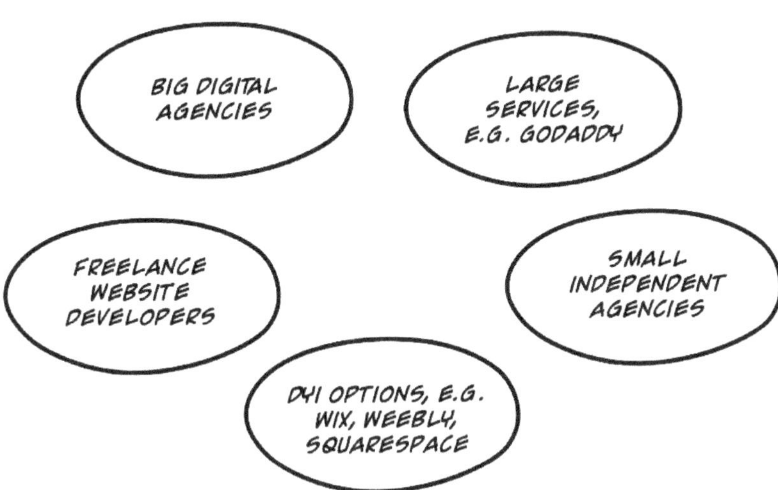

A useful way to do this? Write the down the name of your competitors on Post-It notes, lay them all out, and then start grouping together the similar ones. Have a good look. Are there any logical strategic groups?

Mapping them out – as in the above examples – gives you a better overview of the competitive landscape and helps you understand where you can fill gaps and take advantage of untapped opportunities.

6. Presenting the Competition

When you have done the analysis and mapped the competitive landscape, summarise the information from the analysis in a presentation. This should be a document that anyone, without any prior knowledge of the market, can look at and instantly grasp the the nature of the competition you are dealing with. You can find a made up example in the reader resources at thoranna.is/competition-untangled-reader to give you an idea.

Use whatever is necessary and useful to get the information across and make it easy to understand what each competitor is about, how they are different, where your competitive advantage lies in relation to them, and so on. Use screengrabs, images, quotes, etc. – whatever you find most useful. Remember, this is an in-house document only – so you should not need to worry about anyone outside of your company seeing it. Also remember that a picture is worth a thousand words, so don't just go for a lot of text. Think simple: use images, bullet points, and captions as much
as possible.

7. Ongoing Monitoring and Reviews

You can't just do this work once and then leave it. You need to constantly monitor the competition and update the information when appropriate. Monitoring should be ongoing, and can be done through many of the ways discussed previously in the book – such as an RSS feed of their website, subscribing to their blog or newsletters, following them on social media, etc.

You should also set time aside regularly to do other checks, like visiting their website (not all changes will come up through RSS feeds), doing a Google search for them, visiting their store, restaurant, or whatever it is they have.

Book a regular appointment in your schedule for competitor monitoring. How often you do such monitoring depends on how active the competition is in your market. Thus, competitor monitoring could be something you do daily (as many retail stores would, for example), weekly, monthly, or quarterly. You need to find the right frequency of competitor monitoring for your market, but I would say at the very least do it once a quarter. You should also do a more thorough review of the analysis once a year, and in the first year you may want to also do this after the first six months. Why? Because as soon as you have gone through this, you will find that you are much more aware of things and pick up new information
left, right, and center.

8. Give Them a Run for Their Money

I remember consulting with a young startup once and asking the CEO about the competition. He answered that he didn't pay too much attention to them; he just wanted his team to focus on their own thing. I can totally relate. It is important not to get sucked into obsessing about the competition to the detriment of your own business. In this, like so many other things in life, it's about finding the right balance – of keeping your eyes open but also focusing and not letting the competition distract from your own strategy. By encouraging you to analyse and monitor the competition, I am by no means saying that you should react to their every move. It is the skill of a good business person to know when to react and when to keep going on the same course. However, if you are not aware of what is going on, you will fail to react simply out of ignorance – and that may be fatal for your business. Even the best sprinters on the Olympic track are aware of the other runners – while charging ahead themselves.

I've taken you through why you need to analyse and monitor your competitors, how to determine who they are, what you need to know about them, how to find that information, how to get a helicopter view of your competitor landscape, and how to present the information about your competition to whoever needs to understand the environment your business operates in.

This is where I hand things over to you. Now you have to go ahead and use this information. The time spent reading this book has been utterly useless – unless you act on what I have told you. ;)

It is not those who know things that get ahead – it is those that know and take action. Go take action: analyse your competition, monitor them, and lead your market!

To your marketing success!
xo
Thoranna

P.S. This is not an academic book. It is designed to be accessible to non-marketing specialists and non-academics. Therefore you won't see the text broken up with brackets and names and all those things you would expect in textbooks and journal articles. Many tend to find these references distracting, and it would also take away from the accessible tone of the book.

The book is however firmly based both in academic research and practical knowledge and experience, both my own and that of other warriors in the marketing trenches. At thoranna.is/booksandresources you will find more information about books and resources which underpin my writing and my work on various areas of marketing and branding. I encourage you to check out that link to learn more and open up your marketing world. ;)

About the Author

Thoranna is a marketing specialist with wide-ranging experience dating back to the beginning of the century. (Ehm, although she is not ancient! ;) A self-confessed marketing nerd, she views marketing as not just as her job, but also a passion – as for her it combines the right and left brain, bringing together business and creativity. Marketing also resonates with her as an actress and performer because it is centred around communicating with and influencing people.

Thoranna has worked with global advertising agencies Publicis and McCann Erickson, as well as within the finance and tech industries – particularly with SaaS products. She has worked with a wide spectrum of clients ranging from health companies, baby products, charities, tourism, photography, web services, construction, education, coaching, tech, and more. She holds an MBA with Distinction, focused on strategic marketing, from the University of Westminster in London. She is also a certified digital marketing specialist through DigitalMarketer's extensive training programs.

Soon after the economic collapse of 2008, Thoranna started working with entrepreneurs and startups and has been very involved in her local startup and innovation scene – consulting, mentoring and teaching. Her passion for marketing and entrepreneurship, extensive speaking experience, and media appearances, give her a unique perspective on providing jargon-free, practical marketing advice. Thoranna is not a fan of putting on airs and shrouding herself in incomprehensible jargon to show her expertise, but believes in clear communication. With her, what you see is what you get.

Thoranna lives in Iceland with her husband and two children. Before starting her career in marketing she trained for musical theatre, subsequently working as an actress and singer. Being too straight for the Bohemian life (and today probably too wild for the business world ;), she appeared on television and toured the United Kingdom with the Rocky Horror Show – even meeting the legendary Richard O'Brian. Then, she did a 180-degree turn towards the business world. Thoranna is constantly amazed at how much her former life helps her and those she works with in business!

Find out more at thoranna.is and on social media:

Facebook.com/thoranna.is

Twitter.com/thoranna

LinkedIn.com/in/thorannakristin

Pinterest.com/thoranna

Instagram.com/thorannamarketing